The 102 travelers

left the port of Plymouth, England,

bound for the promise of a new beginning

in a new world . . .

Thanksgiving

A Harvest Celebration

WRITTEN BY **Julie Stiegemeyer**

ILLUSTRATED BY **Renné Benoit**

CONCORDIA PUBLISHING HOUSE • SAINT LOUIS

"Not salted beef again!" Ellen Chilton cried. "That's all we've had for weeks!"

Elizabeth Chilton, her mother, smoothed Ellen's hair. "It's all we have, Ellen," she said. "Be thankful that we are not starving."

As the *Mayflower* rocked the weary travelers, Ellen's father prayed, "O Lord, bless this food which Thou hast provided for our nourishment. If it is Thy will, keep us safe as we journey to our new home. Amen."

Ellen added a silent prayer of her own that they would soon find land.

The Chiltons and other Pilgrim families had set sail from England in September 1620 to begin new lives. Everything they owned was crammed into the belly of this boat. They brought saws and hammers to build new houses, seeds and tools for gardens, cloth and dried beans to trade with the Native Americans. Even two dogs came along.

After their meager supper that night, Ellen snuggled close to her mother as they lay under their quilts. Her father was on deck helping with the watch, looking for land.

Suddenly, they heard shouting and running above deck.

"Land!" someone cried. "We've spotted land!"

After almost two months of seasickness and anticipation, the little band of Pilgrims had crossed the wide ocean and arrived in the New World.

The Chilton family watched with great joy the next day as the *Mayflower* was moored in the safety of the harbor. In time it would be their turn to step onto Plymouth Rock and finally stand on solid ground again.

"Now our work begins," said Ellen's father. "Will you help, Ellen?" Ellen nodded cheerfully. How exciting to help build a new life in a new land!

As the days passed, the men and boys worked quickly to build a shelter. Soon, the Common House became a haven for the Pilgrims, a place where they could live and pray. Others lived on the *Mayflower,* which was still anchored in the harbor. Everyone worked to establish the colony. Ellen helped too. She carried water and gathered wood chips for kindling. She helped her mother and the other women and girls to cook what little food they could gather.

$\mathcal{A}$s the winter wore on, Ellen's mother grew weak from a cough that never seemed to stop.

Ellen helped her mother in the little ways she could. She fed her broth. She bathed her face with a cloth dipped in cool water. And she sang songs to bring a weak smile to her mother's thin face. Still, her mother coughed and coughed.

But others were dying. Her friend's mother. Her father's brother. Life in the New World was supposed to be better, but Ellen was frightened. Sometimes she thought they should have stayed in England.

Ellen prayed every night that God would make her mother well. Slowly, Elizabeth Chilton did regain her health. And Ellen knew God had answered her prayers.

One spring afternoon, as Ellen gathered
kindling for the big fireplace at the Common House,
she spotted something moving in the trees.

She peered closely. It was not a bird. It was not
a rabbit or even a squirrel. It was a man with a dark
face and smiles in his eyes.

Ellen gasped and dropped her armload of wood.
As quickly as she could, she turned and ran to the
safety of the clearing where her father was working.

———

"Papa!" Ellen cried, so startled she could barely speak. She turned and pointed to the man who was following a few steps behind her.

The dark man approached them slowly. In his arms was the wood that Ellen had dropped. "Papa," Ellen whispered, "he helped me!"

No one spoke for a long moment. Then the stranger smiled and tapped his chest. He said, "Sam-o-set." Ellen understood that Samoset must be the man's name.

Samoset and his friends befriended the Pilgrims
and taught them many things about living in the New World:

how to plant corn seeds between
two fish for fertilizer,

where to find wild berries
and turkeys,

how to grow beans
and squash,

how to catch eel and fish,

how to trade with other
native people for furs.

A winter of sickness and death had been followed by a
springtime of hope. Then God provided an abundant summer crop.
The Pilgrims picked berries, harvested vegetables, and salted meat.

When the pumpkins turned from dark green to bright orange, the Pilgrims knew autumn had come to New England. God had sustained them through their difficult first year and provided hope for the winter ahead. With the arrival of autumn, the Pilgrims planned a celebration to thank God for the harvest.

For three days, the Pilgrims gathered with their Native American friends and feasted on turkey, venison, hare, puddings, bread, berries, corn, beans, and squash. The children played games and the adults ate outside under the colored leaves of fall.

At the harvest meal, Ellen helped her mother by carrying dish after dish to the long table. In her heart, she said a little prayer thanking God for helping her mother to get well and for all good things He gives—even salted beef.

———

That thanksgiving meal so many years ago reminds us

that today we, too, thank God for the many blessings He gives.

Some families travel to visit relatives to celebrate their

blessings together on Thanksgiving. Others serve meals at a shelter

for the homeless. Still other families invite friends from other

places to observe Thanksgiving with them in their homes.

——— —

However we celebrate, we thank God for food and drink, shelter and clothing, our minds, our bodies, our health. All that we have comes from our heavenly Father's bountiful hand.

Even better than all these blessings is the gift of Jesus, whose love and promise of salvation fill every day of our lives.

And that is the best reason for giving thanks on Thanksgiving Day and every day!

Praise God, from whom all blessings flow;

Praise Him, all creatures here below;

Praise Him above, O heav'nly host;

Praise Father, Son, and Holy Ghost.